ART IS...

ART IS...

The Metropolitan Museum of Art

New York

"WHAT IS ART?" is a question with no single answer — in fact, this book has nearly two hundred responses.

The answers presented in the following pages are simple observations and reactions to art. All are subjective reflections about what is seen and are open to discussion. Some of the responses given speak to technique, while others are descriptive or invoke emotion. A Michelangelo sketch is practice; a Vermeer painting is mastery. A Nigerian mask is symmetry; a Van Gogh still life is composition. A Babylonian lion is fierce; a Duccio portrait is tender.

Reaching across time and form, from ancient statues to medieval tapestries to Baroque instruments to Impressionist paintings to contemporary costumes, the selected works of art represent The Metropolitan Museum of Art's vast collection of over two million objects and seventeen curatorial departments. Detailed commentary about the works can be found on the Museum's website at www.metmuseum.org.

Because there are no absolute answers—a single work could easily have ten different answers, though for brevity only one was selected—readers are encouraged to observe, to think, to debate, and to develop their own definitions of "art."

Art is practice,

Studies for *The Libyan Sibyl*

Michelangelo Buonarroti, Italian, 1475–1564

Red chalk, 11³/8 × 8⁷/16 in., ca. 1510–11

Purchase, Joseph Pulitzer Bequest, 1924 24.197.2

art is mastery.

Art is a story,

The Death of Socrates (detail)

Jacques-Louis David, French, 1748–1825

Oil on canvas, 51 × 77¹/₄ in., 1787

Catharine Lorillard Wolfe Collection, Wolfe Fund, 1931 31.45

art is an impression.

Bridge over a Pond of Water Lilies
Claude Monet, French, 1840–1926
Oil on canvas, $36^{1}/_{2}$ × 29 in., 1899
H. O. Havemeyer Collection, Bequest of Mrs. H. O. Havemeyer, 1929. 29.100.113

Art is inventive,

Folio from *The Book of the Knowledge of Ingenious Mechanical Devices*
Syria; author: Abu'l Izz Isma'il al-Jazari; copyist: Farkh ibn 'Abd al-Latif
Ink, opaque watercolor, and gold on paper, $11^{13}/_{16} \times 7^3/_4$ in., 1315
Bequest of Cora Timken Burnett, 1956 57.51.23

art is found.

Art is simple,

Head from the figure of a woman
Cycladic, Early Cycladic II
Marble, H. $9^{15}/_{16}$ in., ca. 2700–2500 BC
Gift of Christos G. Bastis 1964 64.246

art is detailed.

"Le Bal" Shoes
Paul Poiret, French, 1879–1944
Made by André Perugia, French, 1893–1977
Silk, glass, leather, L. 10 in., 1924
Purchase, Friends of The Costume Institute Gifts, 2005 2005.192a, b

Art is fierce,

Panel with striding lion (detail)
Mesopotamia (Babylon), Neo-Babylonian period
Glazed brick, H. 38¼ in., ca. 604–562 BC
Fletcher Fund, 1931 31.13.2

art is tender.

Art is symmetry,

Masquerade element: ram head (Omama)
Nigeria; Yoruba Peoples, Owo Group, 17th–19th century
Ivory, wood or coconut shell inlay, H. 6 in.
Gift of Mr. and Mrs. Klaus G. Perls, 1991 1991.17.123

art is composition.

Art is symbolic,

art is descriptive.

The Harvesters (detail)
Pieter Bruegel the Elder, Netherlandish, ca. 1525–1569
Oil on wood, 46⁷/8 × 63³/4 in., 1565
Rogers Fund, 1919 19.164

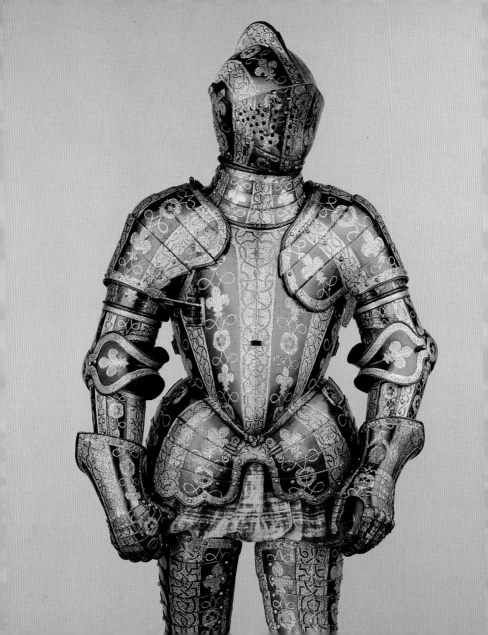

Art is guarded,

Armor of George Clifford, Third Earl of Cumberland (detail)
English (Greenwich), ca. 1585
Steel, etched, blued, and gilded, H. 69 $^{1}/_{2}$ in.
Munsey Fund, 1932 32.130.6

art is uninhibited.

Summer (detail)
Frederick Carl Frieseke, American, 1874–1939
Oil on canvas, 45 3/16 × 57 3/4 in., 1914
George A. Hearn Fund, 1966 66.171

Art is worn,

Dress

Yves Saint Laurent, French, 1936–2008

House of Yves Saint Laurent, Paris (founded 1962)

Wool, fall/winter 1965–66

Gift of Mrs. William Rand, 1969 C.I.69.23

art is heard.

Grand pianoforte
English, ca. 1840
Made by Érard and Company, London
Case by George H. Blake, London
Wood, various materials, L. 97^{1}/$_{4}$ in.
Gift of Mrs. Henry McSweeney, 1959 59.76

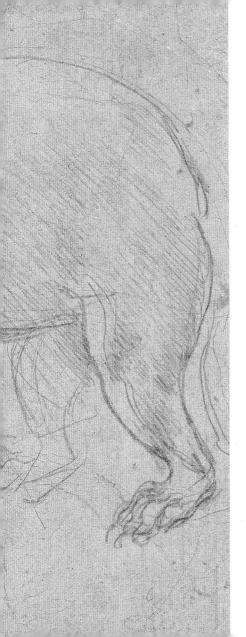

Art is study,

art is craft.

Art is a record,

Art is fanciful,

art is understated.

Fragment of the face of a queen
Egyptian, New Kingdom (Dynasty 18)
Yellow jasper, H. 5 ¹/₈ in., Amarna period (ca. 1353–1336 BC)
Purchase, Edward S. Harkness Gift, 1926 26.7.1396

Art is pattern,

Tunic
Peru (Wari), pre-Columbian period
Camelid hair, 34 × 46 in., 700–850
Gift of Rosetta and Louis Slavitz, 1986 1986.488.3

art is brushstroke.

Wheat Field with Cypresses
Vincent van Gogh, Dutch, 1853–1890
Oil on canvas, 28³/₄ × 36³/₄ in., 1889
Purchase, The Annenberg Foundation Gift, 1993 1993.132

Art is random,

art is ritual.

The Bishop of Assisi Giving a Palm to Saint Clare (detail)
Germany (Nuremberg), ca. 1360
Tempera and gold on oak panel, 13 $^1/_4$ × 8 $^3/_4$ in.
The Cloisters Collection, 1984 1984.343

Art is shape,

art is color.

Sandal
Salvatore Ferragamo, Italian, 1898–1960
House of Salvatore Ferragamo (founded 1929)
Leather, cork, H. 5 1/2 in., 1938
Gift of Salvatore Ferragamo, 1973 1973.282.2

Art is sight,

Scherzo di Follia (Game of Madness)

Pierre-Louis Pierson, French, 1822–1913

Gelatin silver print from glass negative, 15 $^{11}/_{16}$ × 11 $^{3}/_{4}$ in., 1861–67, printed ca. 1930

Gilman Collection, Gift of The Howard Gilman Foundation, 2005 2005.100.198

art is sound.

Guitar

Matteo Sellas, Italian (Venice), ca. 1599–1654

Spruce, bone, parchment, snakewood, ivory, L. 37 $^5/8$ in., ca. 1630–50

Purchase, Clara Mertens Bequest, in memory of André Mertens, 1990 1990.103

Art is delight,

art is sorrow.

Art is history,

art is allegory.

Art is gilded,

art is glazed.

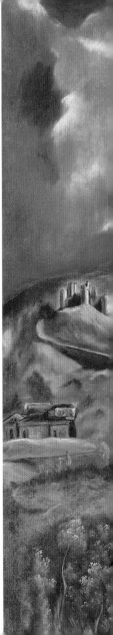

Art is dramatic,

View of Toledo (detail)
El Greco (Domenikos Theotokopoulos), Greek, 1540/41–1614
Oil on canvas, 47³/₄ × 42³/₄ in.
H. O. Havemeyer Collection, Bequest of Mrs. H. O. Havemeyer, 1929 29.100.6

art is serene.

The Lighthouse at Two Lights
Edward Hopper, American, 1882–1967
Oil on canvas, $29\,^1/_2 \times 43\,^1/_4$ in., 1929
Hugo Kastor Fund, 1962 62.95

Art is industrial,

art is homespun.

Sampler

Millsent Connor, American, b. 1789

Embroidered silk on linen, 21 1/8 x 16 1/4 in., 1799

Gift of Edgar William and Bernice Chrysler Garbisch, 1974 1974.42

Art is chiseled,

art is hammered.

Plaque: winged creatures approaching stylized trees (detail)
Iran (said to be from Ziwiye), ca. 8th–7th century BC
Gold, H. 8⁵/₁₆ in.
Purchase, Ann and George Blumenthal Fund, 1954 54.3.5
Rogers Fund, 1962 62.78.1a, b

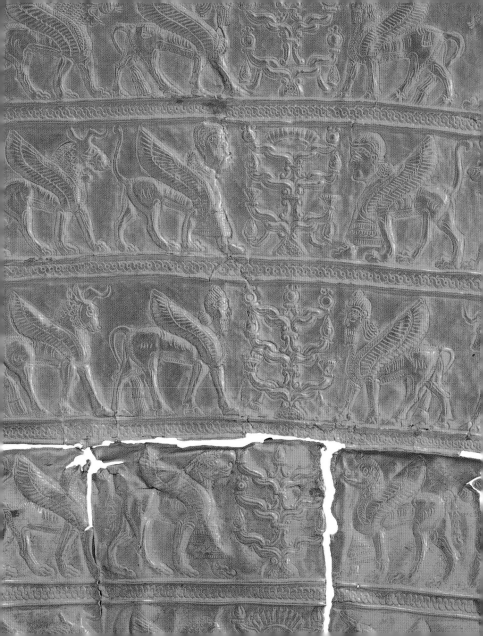

Art is function,

Sewing table

James X. Smith, American, 1806–1888

Cherry, butternut, pine, basswood, sycamore, maple; H. 28 in., 1843

Friends of the American Wing Fund, 1966 66.10.18

art is form.

Commode
Peter Langlois, English, active 1759–1781
Pine and oak with marquetry of satinwood, kingwood,
and other woods on a mahogany ground; gilt bronze, H. 35 in., 1764
Fletcher Fund, 1959 59.127

Art is woven,

art is carved.

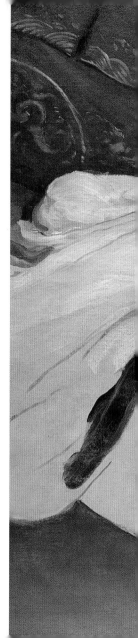

Art is longing,

Repose (detail)

John White Alexander, American, 1856–1915

Oil on canvas, 52 $^1/_4$ × 63 $^5/_8$ in., 1895

Anonymous Gift, 1980 1980.224

art is desire.

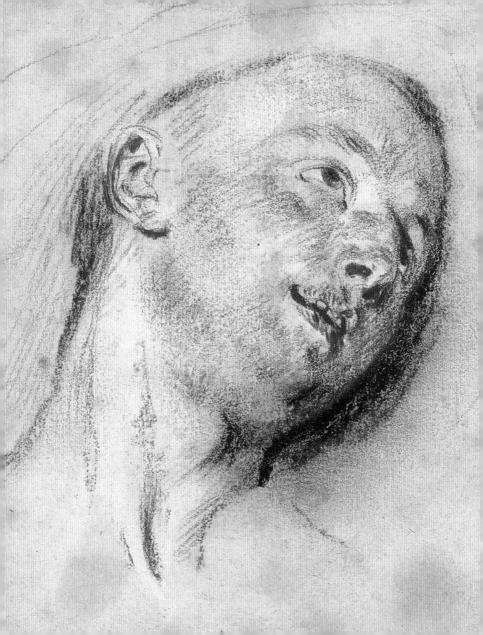

Art is sketch,

art is illumination.

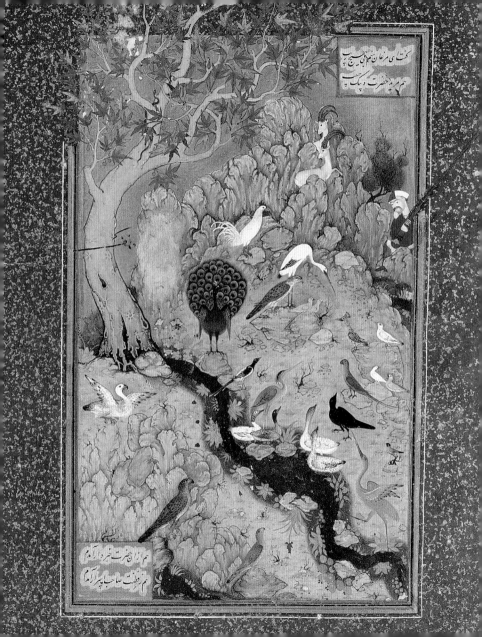

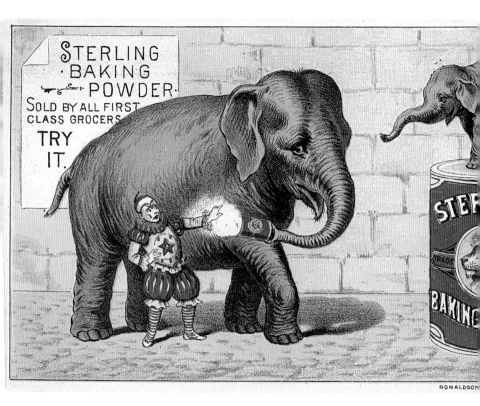

FIVE POINTS, N.Y.

Art is advertisement,

Sterling Baking Powder
American, ca. 1880
Printed by Donaldson Brothers (New York)
Chromolithograph, 3 $^{5}/_{16}$ x 5 $^{5}/_{8}$ in.
The Jefferson R. Burdick Collection, Gift of Jefferson R. Burdick Burdick 17, p.49

art is adaptation.

Art is above your head,

Bedroom from the Sagredo Palace, Venice
Italian (Venice), ca. 1718
Stuccowork probably by Abbondio Stazio, Italian (Massagno), 1675–1745;
and Carpoforo Mazzetti, Italian, ca. 1684–1748; probably after a model
by Gaspare Diziani, Italian (Belluno), 1689–1767
Wood, stucco, marble, glass, H. 25 ft. 2 in.
Rogers Fund, 1906 06.1335.1a–d

art is under your feet.

Art is memory,

art is fantasy.

Pygmalion and Galatea (detail)
Jean-Léon Gérôme, French, 1824–1904
Oil on canvas, 35 X 27 in., ca. 1890
Gift of Louis C. Raegner, 1927 27.200

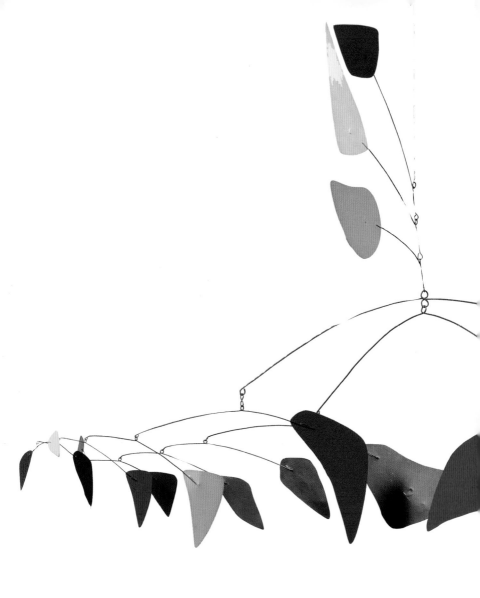

Art is moving,

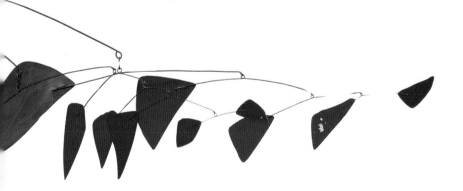

art is still.

Still Life with Apples and a Pot of Primroses (detail)
Paul Cézanne, French, 1839–1906
Oil on canvas, 28 3/4 × 36 3/8 in., ca. 1890
Bequest of Sam A. Lewisohn, 1951 51.112.1

Art is monumental,

art is miniature.

Art is restrained,

Seated harp player
Cycladic, late Early Cycladic I–Early Cycladic II
Marble, H. 11 $^1/_2$ in., ca. 2800–2700 BC
Rogers Fund, 1947 47.100.1

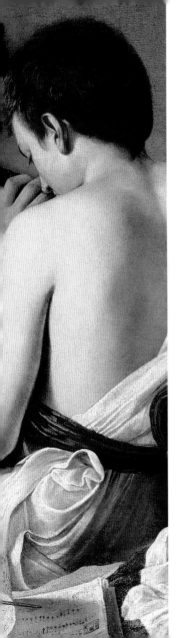

art is sensuous.

The Musicians (detail)
Caravaggio (Michelangelo Merisi), Italian, 1571–1610
Oil on canvas, $36^1/_4 \times 46^5/_8$ in., ca. 1595
Rogers Fund, 1952 52.81

Art is useful,

art is whimsical.

Art is skill,

art is chance.

Four playing cards from a set of fifty-two

South Netherlandish, ca. 1470–80

Pasteboard with pen and ink, tempera, applied gold and silver, $5^3/8 \times 2^3/4$ in.

The Cloisters Collection, 1983 1983.515.1-.52

Art is didactic,

art is expressive.

Improvisation 27 (Garden of Love II)
Vasily Kandinsky, French (b. Russia), 1866–1944
Oil on canvas, 47³/₈ × 55¹/₄ in., 1912
Alfred Stieglitz Collection, 1949 49.70.1
© Artists Rights Society (ARS), New York / ADAGP, Paris

Art is ornamental,

Rapier of Christian II, Elector of Saxony (detail)
German (Dresden), 1606
Hilt by Israel Schuech, German, active 1590–1610
Blade by Juan Martinez, Spanish
Steel, bronze, jewels, gold, enamel, L. 48 in.
Fletcher Fund, 1970 1970.77

art is unadorned.

Art is collage,

art is mosaic.

Fragment of a floor mosaic with a personification of Ktisis
Byzantine, 500–550 with modern restoration
Marble and glass, 59 1/2 × 78 5/8 in.
Harris Brisbane Dick Fund and Fletcher Fund, 1998 1998.69
Purchase, Lila Acheson Wallace Gift,
Dodge Fund, and Rogers Fund, 1999 1999.99

Art is rendered,

Four Tulips: Boter man (Butter Man), Joncker (Nobleman),
Grote geplumaceerde (The Great Plumed One), and Voorwint (With the Wind)
Jakob Marrel, German, 1613/14–1681
Watercolor on vellum, 13³/₁₆ x 17⁵/₁₆ in., before 1681
Rogers Fund, 1968 68.66

Joncker.　　　　*grote geplumaceerde.*　　　　*Voorwint.*

art is stitched.

Art is structured,

Chapter house from Notre-Dame-de-Ponaut
French (Aquitaine), 12th century
Limestone, H. 37 ft. 9 in.
The Cloisters Collection, 1935 35.50

art is dynamic.

Autumn Rhythm (Number 30)
Jackson Pollock, American, 1912–1956
Enamel on canvas, 8 ft. $^3/_4$ in. × 17 ft. $^1/_4$ in., 1950
George A. Hearn Fund, 1957 57.92
© Pollock-Krasner Foundation / Artists Rights Society (ARS), New York

Paulus Be Seim.   A° 1546.

Art is competition,

art is conquest.

Art is young,

Manuel Osorio Manrique de Zuñiga (1784–1792)
Goya (Francisco de Goya y Lucientes), Spanish, 1746–1828
Oil on canvas, 50 × 40 in.
The Jules Bache Collection, 1949 49.7.41

art is old.

Art is figurative,

art is abstract.

Art is philosophy,

art is belief.

The Annunciation (detail)
Botticelli (Alessandro di Mariano Filipepi), Italian (Florence), 1444/45–1510
Tempera and gold on wood, $7^{1}/_{2}$ × $12^{3}/_{8}$ in., ca. 1485
Robert Lehman Collection, 1975 1975.1.74

Art is self,

art is madness.

Art is line,

Studies of a Horse in Profile

Eugène Delacroix, French, 1798–1863

Pencil on gray-beige wove paper (probably a sheet from a sketchbook), 5 5/8 × 8 7/8 in., 1825–31

Robert Lehman Collection, 1975 1975.1.612

art is point.

Art is pride,

art is humiliation.

Aristotle Ridden by Phyllis
South Netherlandish, late 14th century
Bronze, H. 13 1/4 in.
Robert Lehman Collection, 1975 1975.1.1416

Art is lush,

A Vase of Flowers (detail)

Margareta Haverman, Dutch, active by 1716–died 1722 or later

Oil on wood, 31 1/4 x 23 3/4 in., 1716

Purchase, 1871 71.6

art is spare.

Art is hunger,

The Repast of the Lion (detail)
Henri Rousseau (le Douanier), French, 1844–1910
Oil on canvas, 44³/₄ × 63 in., ca. 1907
Bequest of Sam A. Lewisohn, 1951 51.112.5

art is nourishment.

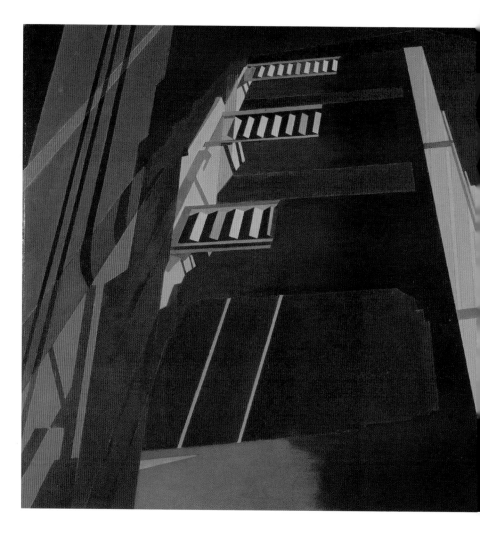

Art is precision,

art is juxtaposition.

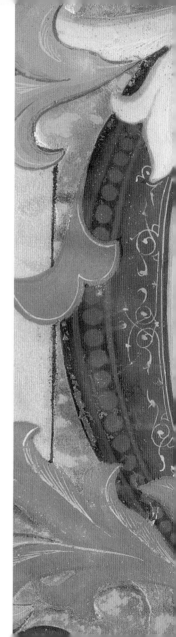

Art is saintly,

art is sinful.

Bacchanal with a Wine Vat (detail)
Andrea Mantegna, Italian, 1430/31–1506
Engraving and drypoint, 11³/₄ × 17¹/₄ in., ca. 1470–90
Purchase, Rogers Fund, The Charles Engelhard Foundation Gift, and
The Elisha Whittelsey Collection, The Elisha Whittelsey Fund, 1986 1986.1159

Art is translucent,

art is solid.

Limestone sarcophagus: the Amathus sarcophagus

Cypriot, Archaic period

Limestone, L. 93 ¹/₈ in., 2nd quarter 5th century BC

The Cesnola Collection, Purchased by subscription, 1874–76 74.51.2453

Art is on a wall,

art is in a closet.

Evening dress (detail)
Hubert de Givenchy, French, b. 1927
House of Givenchy (founded 1952)
Silk, feathers, 1968–69
Gift of Mrs. Claus von Bülow, 1971 1971.79.4

Art is creation,

art is destruction.

Art is angular,

Plant stand

Otto Prutscher, Austrian, 1880–1949

Made by Beissbarth and Hoffmann, Germany

Wood, metal, paint, H. 36$^{1}/_{2}$ in., 1903

Purchase, Lila Acheson Wallace Gift, 1993 1993.303a–f

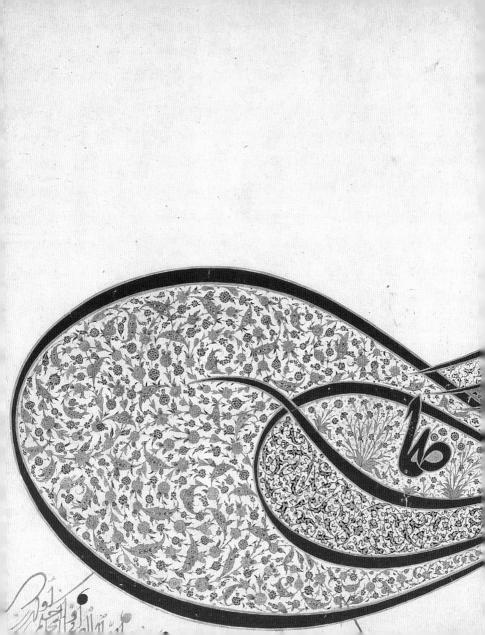

art is sinuous.

Tughra (Official Signature) of Sultan Suleiman the Magnificent (r. 1520–1566) (detail)
Turkey, Ottoman period
Ink, opaque watercolor, and gold on paper, 20^1/$_2$ x 25^3/$_8$ in., ca. 1555
Rogers Fund, 1938 38.149.1

Art is printed,

art is painted.

Lilacs in a Window (Vase de Lilas à la Fênetre)
Mary Cassatt, American, 1844–1926
Oil on canvas, 24³/₁₆ x 20¹/₈ in., ca. 1880–83
Partial and Promised Gift of Susan and Douglas Dillon, 1997 1997.207

Art is real,

art is imaginary.

Art is sacred,

Mosque lamp for the mausoleum of Amir Aydakin al-'Ala'i al-Bunduqdar
Egypt (probably Cairo), Mamluk period (1250–1517)
Glass; blown, folded foot; applied handles; enameled and gilded, H. 10 3/8 in., ca. 1285
Gift of J. Pierpont Morgan, 1917 17.190.985

art is profane.

Art is regal,

art is humble.

Art is seascape,

art is cityscape.

Financial District, From the Hotel Bossert
Samuel H. Gottscho, American, 1875–1971
Gelatin silver print, 6⁹/₁₆ × 9⁷/₁₆ in., 1933, printed later
Purchase, Florance Waterbury Bequest, 1970 1970.660.11

Art is narrative,

art is myth.

Diana and Actaeon (Diana Surprised in Her Bath) (detail)
Camille Corot, French, 1796–1875
Oil on canvas, 61 ^{5}/8 × 44 ^{3}/8 in., 1836
Robert Lehman Collection, 1975 1975.1.162

Art is atmospheric,

The Flatiron

Edward Steichen, American (b. Luxembourg), 1879–1973

Gum bichromate over platinum print, $18^{13}/_{16} \times 15^{1}/_{8}$ in., 1904, printed 1909

Alfred Stieglitz Collection, 1933   33.43.39

art is ethereal.

Landscape—Scene from "Thanatopsis"
Asher Brown Durand, American, 1796–1886
Oil on canvas, 39 1/2 × 61 in., 1850
Gift of J. Pierpont Morgan, 1911 11.156

Art is a glance,

art is a gaze.

Art is instruction,

art is construction.

Dress

Ji Eon Kang, American, b. 1973

Silk, metal, L. 29^{1}/$_{4}$ in., spring/summer 1997

Gift of Richard Martin, 1997 1997.250.6

Art is documentary,

art is legend.

Art is embroidered,

Textile with animals, birds, and flowers
Eastern Central Asia, late 12th–14th century
Silk embroidery on plain-weave silk, $14^5/8 \times 14^7/8$ in.
Rogers Fund, 1988 1988.296

art is etched.

Comb Morion (detail)
German (Brunswick?), ca. 1560–65
Etched steel, H. 12¹/₂ in.
Purchase, The Sulzberger Foundation Inc. and
Ronald S. Lauder Gifts, 1999 1999.62

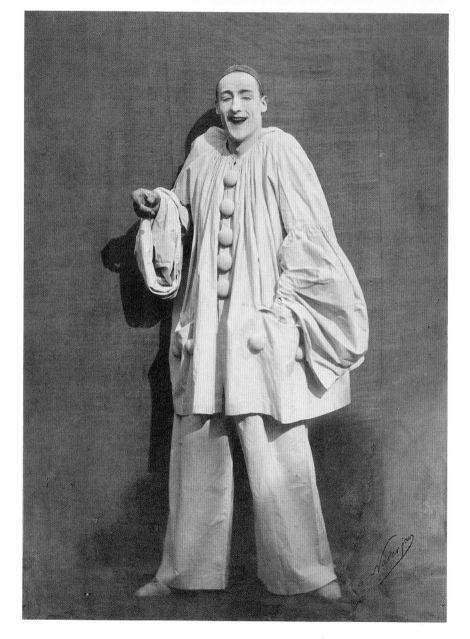

Art is comedy,

art is tragedy.

Grave stele of a little girl (detail)
Greek, classical, ca. 450–440 BC
Marble, Parian, H. 31 1/2 in.
Fletcher Fund, 1927 27.45

Art is bejeweled,

Automaton
Switzerland, ca. 1820
Gold, enamel, diamond, ruby, L. 2$^{7}/_{16}$ in.
Gift of Murtogh D. Guinness, 1976 1976.285.2a–c

art is austere.

Art is war,

art is victory.

Art is honesty,

art is chicanery.

The Fortune Teller (detail)
Georges de La Tour, French, 1593–1653
Oil on canvas, 40¹/₈ × 48⁵/₈ in., probably 1630s
Rogers Fund, 1960 60.30

Diary p. 198
R. Dabney, Powhatan C.H. Va 1852

F R O N T.

0   10   20   30

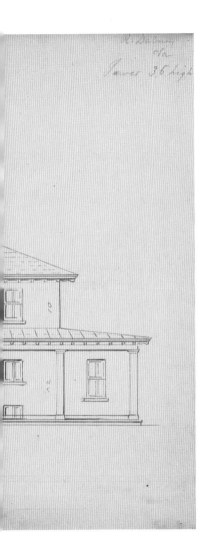

Art is drafted,

House for R. Dabney, Powhatan, Virginia (front elevation)
Alexander Jackson Davis, American, 1803–1892
Ink and wash, $9^{1}/_{4} \times 13^{5}/_{8}$ in., 1856
Harris Brisbane Dick Fund, 1924 24.66.1405(52)

art is sculpted.

Art is interpretation,

art is another interpretation.

Art is common,

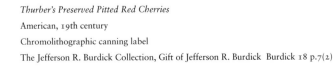

Thurber's Preserved Pitted Red Cherries

American, 19th century

Chromolithographic canning label

The Jefferson R. Burdick Collection, Gift of Jefferson R. Burdick Burdick 18 p.7(2)

art is sublime.

Art is sport,

art is theater.

The Cathedrals of Broadway
Florine Stettheimer, American, 1871–1944
Oil on canvas, 60¹/₈ x 50¹/₈ in., 1929
Gift of Ettie Stettheimer, 1953 53.24.3

Art is pious,

Reliquary bust of a female saint
South Netherlandish (possibly Brussels), ca. 1520–30
Oak, paint, gilding, H. 16^{11}/$_{16}$ in.
The Cloisters Collection, 1959 59.70

art is provocative.

Art is mannered,

art is photographic.

Georgia O'Keeffe

Alfred Stieglitz, American, 1864–1946

Palladium print, $4^5/8 \times 3^9/16$ in., 1918

Gift of Georgia O'Keeffe, through the generosity of

The Georgia O'Keeffe Foundation and Jennifer and Joseph Duke, 1997

1997.61.25

Art is a journey,

Journey to Abydos, Tomb of Pairy (detail)
Egyptian, New Kingdom (Dynasty 18)
Tempera on paper, facsimile: 11 × 28 1/8 in., ca. 1390–1352 BC
Rogers Fund, 1930 30.4.96

art is an adventure.

Untitled (Cowboy)
Richard Prince, American, b. 1949
Chromogenic print, 50 × 70 in., 1989
Purchase, The Horace W. Goldsmith Foundation Gift through Joyce and
Robert Menschel and Jennifer and Joseph Duke Gift, 2000 2000.272
© Richard Prince

Art is warm,

art is cool.

Art is vanity,

Lady Lilith (detail)

Dante Gabriel Rossetti, English, 1828–1882

Watercolor and gouache, on paper, 20³/₁₆ × 17⁵/₁₆ in., 1867

Rogers Fund, 1908 08.162.1

art is self-sacrifice.

Joan of Arc (detail)
Jules Bastien-Lepage, French, 1848–1884
Oil on canvas, 8 ft. 4 in. × 9 ft. 2 in., 1879
Gift of Erwin Davis, 1889 89.21.1

Art is an emblem,

Bowl with the arms of Pope Julius II and the Manzoli of Bologna
surrounded by putti, cornucopiae, satyrs, dolphins, birds
Workshop of Giovanni Maria Vasaro, Italian, active early 16th century
Majolica (tin-glazed earthenware), D. 12$^{13}/_{16}$ in., 1508
Robert Lehman Collection, 1975 1975.1.1015

art is an icon.

Portable icon with the Virgin Eleousa
Byzantine (Constantinople), early 14th century
Miniature mosaic set in wax on wood panel,
with gold, multicolored stones, and gilded copper; $4^{7}/_{16} \times 3^{3}/_{8}$ in.
Gift of John C. Weber, in honor of Philippe de Montebello, 2008 2008.352

Art is reflection,

Fur Traders Descending the Missouri (detail)
George Caleb Bingham, American, 1811–1879
Oil on canvas, 29 × 36¹/₂ in., 1845
Morris K. Jesup Fund, 1933 33.61

art is perspective.

Piazza San Marco
Canaletto (Giovanni Antonio Canal), Italian (Venice), 1697–1768
Oil on canvas, 27 × 44 1/4 in.
Purchase, Mrs. Charles Wrightsman Gift, 1988 1988.162

Art is calligraphy,

Night-Shining White (detail)

Han Gan, Chinese, active ca. 742–756

Handscroll; ink on paper, 12¹/₈ x 13³/₈ in., Tang dynasty (618–907), ca. 750

Purchase, The Dillon Fund Gift, 1977 1977.78

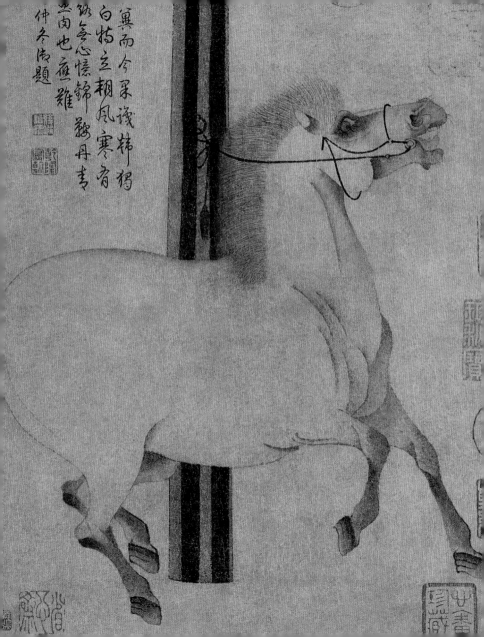

Questa letera A sicaua del tondo e del suo quadro: la gã
ba da man drita uol esser grossa dele noue parti luna de
lalteza. La gamba senistra uol esser la mita de la gãba gros
sa. La gamba de mezo uol esser la terza parte de la gamba
grossa. La largheza de dita letera cadauna gamba per me
zo de la crosiera, quella di mezo alquanto piu bassa com
me uedi qui per li diametri segnati.

art is type.

Page from *Divina proportione*
Fra Luca Pacioli, Italian, died ca. 1514
After Leonardo da Vinci, Italian, 1452–1519
Published by Paganinus de Paganinus, Venice
Book with woodcut illustrations, 11⁵/₈ × 8¹/₄ in., 1509
Rogers Fund, 1919 19.50

Art is polished,

Presentation vase
Thomas Fletcher, American, 1787–1866,
and Sidney Gardiner, American, 1787–1827
Silver, H. 23⁷/₁₆ in., 1824
Purchase, Louis V. Bell and Rogers Funds;
Anonymous and Robert G. Goelet Gifts; and
Gifts of Fenton L. B. Brown and of the grandchildren
of Mrs. Ranson Spaford Hooker, in her memory, by exchange, 1982
1982.4a, b

The Merchants of Pearl Street, New York,

TO THE HON. DEWITT CLINTON,

Whose claim to the proud title of Public Benefactor
is founded on those monumental works,

The Northern and Western CANALS.

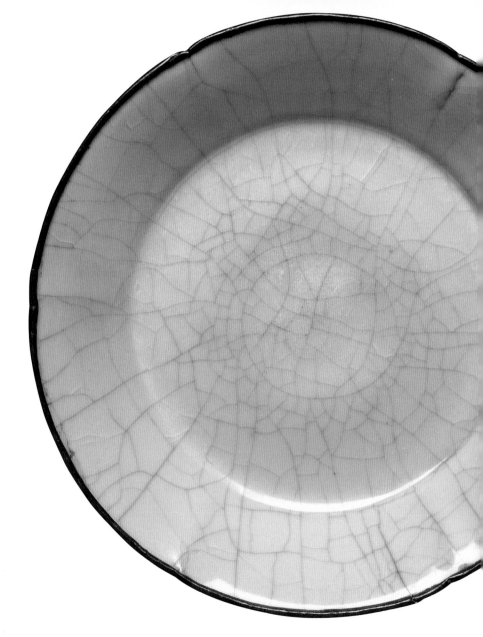

art is crackled.

Dish

Chinese, Southern Song dynasty (1127–1279)

Stoneware with crackled blue glaze, D. 8 5/8 in.

Fletcher Fund, 1924 24.172.1

Art is seen,

Evening dress
American or European, 1884–86
Silk
Gift of Mrs. J. Randall Creel IV, 1963   C.I.63.23.3a, b

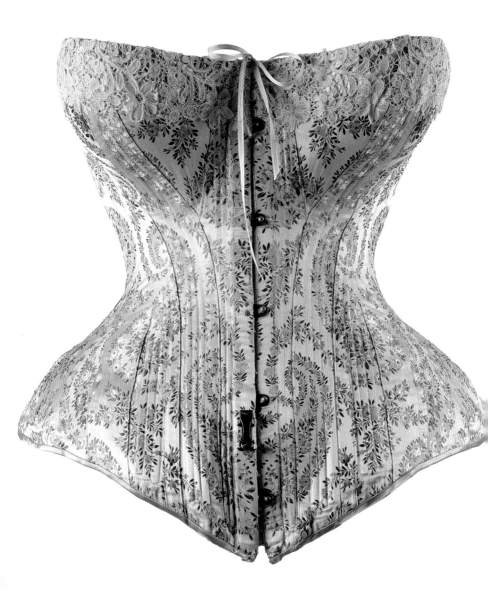

art is hidden.

Art is portrait,

art is landscape.

Jalais Hill, Pontoise (detail)
Camille Pissarro, French, 1830–1903
Oil on canvas, 34^1/$_4$ × 45^1/$_4$ in., 1867
Bequest of William Church Osborn, 1951 51.30.2

Art is organic,

Conch shell trumpet
Philippines
Shell *(triton titonis)*, L. 13 1/2 in.
The Crosby Brown Collection of Musical Instruments, 1889 89.4.3417

art is fabricated.

"*Patriot*" Radio
Norman Bel Geddes, American, 1893–1958
Made by Emerson Radio and Phonograph Corp., New York
Catalin, H. 8 in., ca. 1940
John C. Waddell Collection, Gift of John C. Waddell, 2001   2001.722.11

Art is conceptual,

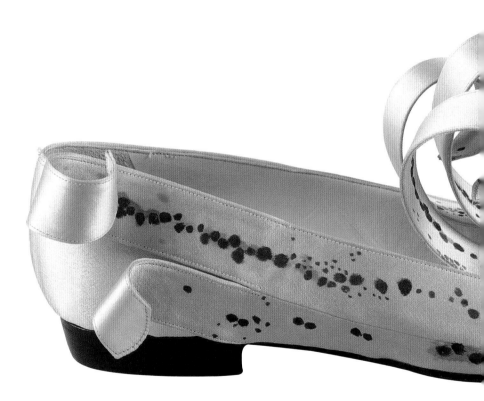

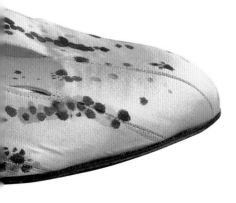

art is representation.

Art is geometric,

Temple Gardens
Paul Klee, German (b. Switzerland), 1879–1940
Gouache and traces of ink on paper, $7^1/_4$ × $10^1/_4$ in., 1920
The Berggruen Klee Collection, 1987 1987.455.2

art is arabesque.

Art is rhythm,

Side drum
Ernest Vogt, American, 19th century
Wood, calf skin, rope, D. 16^7/$_8$ in., ca. 1864
The Crosby Brown Collection of Musical Instruments, 1889 89.4.2162

art is dance.

The Dance Class (detail)

Edgar Degas, French, 1834–1917

Oil on canvas, 32⁷/₈ × 30³/₈ in., 1874

Bequest of Mrs. Harry Payne Bingham, 1986 1987.47.1

Art is built,

art is abandoned.

Art is fable,

Detail of a cabinet depicting "The Woodman and the Serpent" from *Aesop's Fables*
Made by Galleria dei Lavori, Italian (Florence), 1606–23
Oak and poplar veneered with various exotic hardwoods, with ebony moldings and
plaques of marble, slate (paragon); pietre dure work consisting of colored marbles, rock
crystal, and various hardstones; L. 38^1/8 in.
Wrightsman Fund, 1988 1988.19

art is parable.

Art is depth,

art is illusion.

Art is attentive,

The Little Fourteen-year-old Dancer
Edgar Degas, French, 1834–1917
Bronze, partially tinted, with cotton skirt and satin hair-ribbon; wood base,
H. 38¹/₂ in., executed ca. 1880, cast in 1922
H.O. Havemeyer Collection, Bequest of Mrs. H.O. Havemeyer, 1929
29.100.370

art is weary.

Seated figure
Mali (Djenné), 13th century
Terracotta, H. 10 in.
Purchase, Buckeye Trust and Mr. and Mrs. Milton F. Rosenthal Gifts, Joseph Pulitzer
Bequest and Harris Brisbane Dick and Rogers Funds, 1981 1981.218

Art is suggestive,

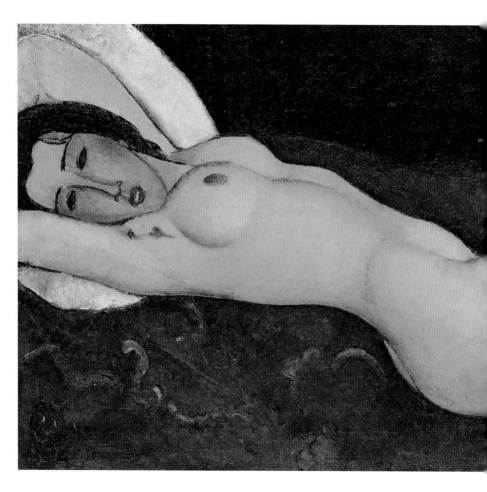

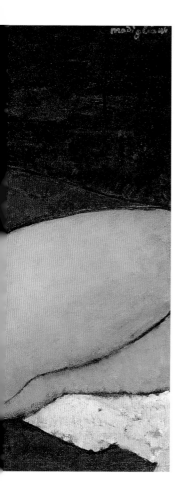

art is revealing.

Reclining Nude
Amedeo Modigliani, Italian, 1884–1920
Oil on canvas, 23 7/8 × 36 1/2 in., 1917
The Mr. and Mrs. Klaus G. Perls Collection, 1997 1997.149.9

Art is observation,

Ocean Life (detail)

Christian Schussele, American, 1824–1879

James M. Sommerville, American, 1825–1899

Watercolor, gouache, graphite, and gum arabic on off-white wove paper, 19 × 27⁷/₁₆ in.

Gift of Mr. and Mrs. Erving Wolf, in memory of Diane R. Wolf, 1977 1977.181

art is imagination.

Published by The Metropolitan Museum of Art

The Metropolitan Museum of Art
1000 Fifth Avenue
New York, NY 10028
212.570.3894
www.metmuseum.org

Produced by the Department of Special Publications, The Metropolitan Museum of Art: Robie Rogge, Publishing Manager; Mimi Tribble, Editor; Mary Wong, Senior Production Specialist. Photography by The Metropolitan Museum of Art Photograph Studio.

Cover designed by Seoyeon Sally Lee. Interior designed by Kate Kennedy.

Printed in Hong Kong

16 15 14   10 9 8 7 6 5 4

ISBN: 978-1-58839-447-7